GOD Is Like...

Three Parables for Children

by Julie Walters   *watercolors by* Thea Kliros

WATERBROOK
PRESS

GOD IS LIKE...
Published by WATERBROOK PRESS
5446 North Academy Boulevard, Suite 200
Colorado Springs, Colorado 80918
A division of Random House, Inc.

Scripture taken from the *Holy Bible, New International Version*®.
NIV®. Copyright © 1973, 1978, 1984 by International Bible
Society. Used by permission of Zondervan Publishing House.
All rights reserved.

ISBN 1-57856-246-5

Copyright © 2000 by Julie Walters

Illustrations copyright © 2000 by Thea Kliros

Printed in the United States of America
2000—First Edition

10 9 8 7 6 5 4 3 2 1

For my grandchildren

Anne, Elizabeth, Rebecca, Anna, Maria, Mark, Melissa,

Monica, Peter John, John Michael, and Jack—J.W.

To David Douglas—T.K.

The ROCK

This is

the rock...

...that was by a lake.

In the spring,
the waves splashed
over the rock...

...and washed away the sand.

But the **rock** stayed the same.

In the summer, the sun shone so hot
that the wildflowers wilted.
But the ROCK stayed the same.

In fall, the winds whisked the leaves from the trees and scattered the seeds.

The rain poured down.

The sand became soggy-wet.

But the **rock** stayed the same.

In winter,

the cold air changed the rain into snow

and the lake water into ice.

But the **rock** did not change.

It stayed the same.

One summer day,
a boy climbed
on the **rock**.

He jumped
up and down.
He rocked
back and forth.

But the **rock** did not wiggle or move.
It stayed steadfastly in its place.

He pretended that
the **rock** was his
strong, steady ship.
It carried him
through high waves
and howling winds.

The boy pulled the **rock**.

He pushed on the **rock**.

But the **rock** would not wiggle or move.
It stayed steadfastly in its place.

The boy crouched behind the rock.

He peeked around one side.

He peeked around the other side.

He pretended that the **rock** hid him

and saved him from

a roaring lion of the jungle.

The boy built sand castles
with a paper cup.
He smoothed out roads.
He dug rivers
and filled them with water.

He used twigs
for people.

He pretended that the **rock**
was a big mountain
that protected
his castles and people

from dangers on the other side.

Every summer
the boy came back
to the rock
by the lake.

Every year
the boy was bigger.

But the **rock** stayed the same.

I wonder...

could **God** be like a rock?

Yes, **God** our Father is like a **rock**.
He never changes.
His love is always there
and always the same.

"*I love you, O* LORD, *my strength.*

The LORD *is my rock...*"

PSALM 18 : 1 - 2

A SPARK
of Light

A spark of light shone in the darkness.

It grew bigger...

...and bigger, until...

Whiff!

It burst into flame.

The flame lit a candle.

The candle gave its light
to another candle.

And that candle
gave its light
to another candle.

One, two, three, four, five.
Look at all that light!

Then the flame
gave its light to some logs.
And guess what happened?

Yes, a campfire.
But what is that
            moving in the darkness?

It's coming closer!

It's the girl's father.
In the **light**
he doesn't look
scary at all.

Together they listened
to the campfire
crackle and snap.

Sparks shot high
into the air.

The girl pretended
that she was an Indian
tracking in the woods.

She lost her way

until a spark

of light in the sky

pointed the way

back to the campfire.

The girl smelled the smoky air
as she roasted marshmallows.

She watched the movement of the fire.

The fire changed
one marshmallow
into a
flaming torch.

The girl pretended
that she rescued
some friends
who were lost
in the darkness of a cave.

She held the torchlight high
so they could follow it back
to the safety of the campfire.

The girl let the fire burn
the rest of the marshmallow
off the stick
until it was clean.

The girl touched
the point
of her stick.

Ouch! It was still hot.

She pretended that she was a great doctor.

She sterilized her sharp instruments
in the fire before removing
a splinter from a puppy's paw.

The fire warmed the girl
as she slept through the night.
It kept away the wild animals
in the forest.

When the girl awoke,
the fire was almost out.
It had turned the logs into
smoke and ashes.

The girl squinted up at the morning sun.

It was so bright!

It lit up everything.

I wonder...

could God be like
the light?

Yes, Jesus, the Son of God,
is like the light
that lights up all our darkness.

Jesus said,

"I am the light of the world..."

JOHN 8:12

A BREATH
of Wind

A breath of **wind**

stirred the ashes of a campfire.

Whiff—

a tiny spark burst into flame.

Then the **wind** swooped up
high into the treetops,

swishing through the leaves,
swaying the branches back and forth.

A flying squirrel glided

from one tree limb to another.

The **wind** held him up.

The wind quickened.

It whipped up
white-capped waves on the lake.

It pushed the clouds across the sky.

It rushed at a puffy white dandelion.
It whisked off its downy seeds,

sailed them through the air,
and planted them far away.

One of the seeds,

like a tiny parachute,

drifted down past the boy.

He took a deep breath of air,
and—whoooh—blew the seed
high into the sky.

The boy pretended
  that he was fastened to a parachute,
  floating high above the trees,

going wherever the **wind** sent him.

The boy walked down to the lake
and pushed his sailboat
through the water.

He blew at it until

he was out of breath.

It moved slowly.

Then it stopped.

But a breeze filled the sail
and carried his boat
over the ripples.

The boy pretended

that he was in a sailboat race.

The **wind** swept him

around the last buoy

and to the finish line.

He won!

The boy sat on a rock.

He took a balloon out of his pocket
and blew his breath into it.

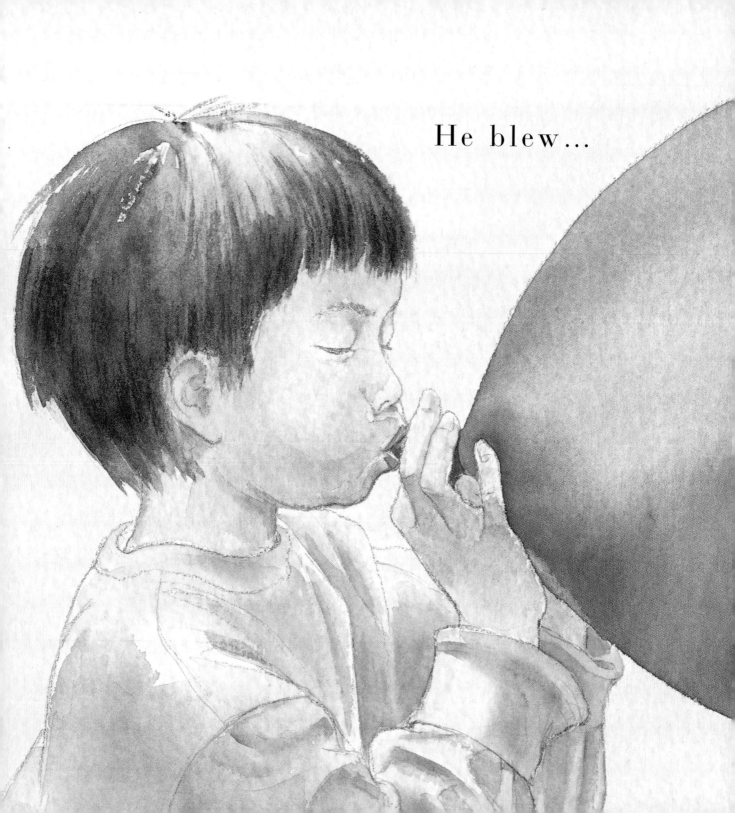

He blew...

...and blew.

He pretended that he was a lifeguard
like the one on the high lookout chair
and breathed his breath
into a little boy
and saved his life.

The boy could not see the **wind**,
but he could see the clouds
sweeping across the sky.

The **wind** brought to him
the smell of flowers.

He could feel the coolness
of the **wind** on his face
and hear it whisper to him
through the trees.

And when the **wind** blew hard,

he let it push him home.

I wonder...
could **God** be like the **wind**?

Yes, God's Spirit
is like the **wind**.
He does His work
without being seen.

"The wind blows wherever it pleases...
So it is with everyone
born of the Spirit."